Farm Machines
at Work

# Sprayers
## Go to Work

Emma Carlson Berne

D1446148

Lerner Publications ◆ Minneapolis

To Bruce Gaskins, for patiently explaining the finer points of farm equipment and for answering many phone calls

Lerner Publications Company
A division of Lerner Publishing Group, Inc.
241 First Avenue North
Minneapolis, MN 55401 USA

For reading levels and more information, look up this title at www.lernerbooks.com.

Main body text set in Billy Infant Semibold 17/23.
Typeface provided by SparkyType.


**Library of Congress Cataloging-in-Publication Data**

Names: Berne, Emma Carlson, author.
Title: Sprayers go to work / Emma Carlson Berne.
Description: Minneapolis : Lerner Publications, 2018. | Series: Farm machines at work | Includes
    bibliographical references and index.
Identifiers: LCCN 2017053442 (print) | LCCN 2017055686 (ebook) | ISBN 9781541526099 (eb pdf) |
    ISBN 9781541526037 (lb : alk. paper) | ISBN 9781541527706 (pb : alk. paper)
Subjects: LCSH: Spraying equipment—Juvenile literature. | Spraying and dusting in agriculture—Juvenile
    literature.
Classification: LCC S694 (ebook) | LCC S694 .B47 2018 (print) | DDC 681/.7631—dc23

LC record available at https://lccn.loc.gov/2017053442

Manufactured in the United States of America
1-44571-35502-3/20/2018

# TABLE OF CONTENTS

# 1
# FARMS NEED SPRAYERS

Many farmers grow plants called crops. Spraying fertilizers on crops can help them grow strong. But weeds and insects can hurt crops.

Some farmers use chemicals to protect their crops from weeds and insects. Herbicides kill weeds. Insecticides stop insects from eating a farmer's crops.

Farmers spray these chemicals on crops with sprayers. Sprayers can be small or large.

Small sprayers look a little like a backpack with a hose and nozzle attached.

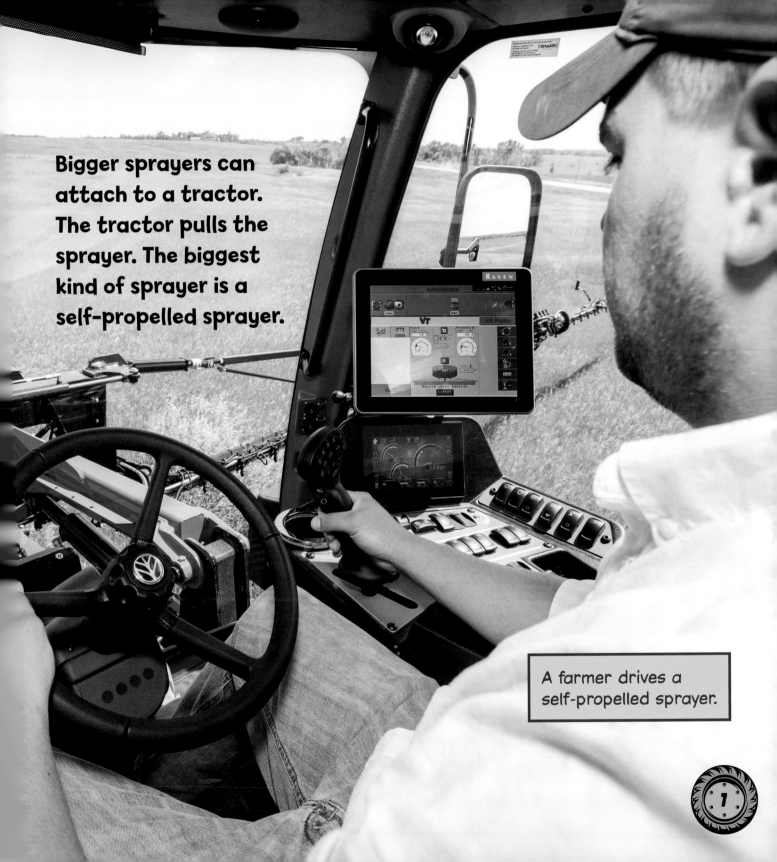

Bigger sprayers can attach to a tractor. The tractor pulls the sprayer. The biggest kind of sprayer is a self-propelled sprayer.

A farmer drives a self-propelled sprayer.

7

# 2

# EXPLORE
## THE SPRAYER

A self-propelled sprayer has a cab and big wheels. A chemical tank sits on the sprayer.

Huge arms called booms reach out from either side of the sprayer. Booms can be on the front or the back of the sprayer.

Booms have nozzles on them. A pump inside the sprayer pushes chemicals from the tank out to the nozzles.

The farmer sits in the cab and drives the sprayer around her field. The chemicals spray from the nozzles onto the crops.

A farmer controls the sprayer using buttons inside the cab.

# 3 SPRAYERS ON THE FARM

Farmers use sprayers while crops are growing. They spray fertilizers, herbicides, and pesticides.

Some crops grow to be big. If crops are big enough, they block the weeds on their own. Farmers may need to spray these crops with herbicides only once.

Farmers may need to spray smaller crops more than once.

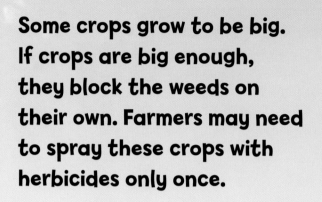

Farmers spray insecticides on a plant's leaves to keep bugs away.

Farmers often need to spray insecticides on crops many times. Moths and grasshoppers are just a couple of the insects that can eat a farmer's crops.

When it is not in use, the sprayer might be stored in a barn. The big boom arms fold up and in. Then they will not take up as much space.

# SPRAYERS YESTERDAY, TODAY, AND TOMORROW

Farmers have used sprayers on their crops for about 150 years. The first sprayers were small and operated by hand.

A steam engine sprayer was carried on a cart pulled by horses or a tractor.

Later, horses pulled sprayers. Then sprayers were steam-powered. They used a steam engine to work.

Organic farm crops are grown with fertilizers that come from plants or animals.

Most modern farms use mechanical sprayers. But not all farms use the same kinds of chemicals. Organic farms use chemicals found in nature.

The newest sprayers can keep track of where they have sprayed. The nozzles on the booms are even better at spraying only where chemicals are needed. These sprayers help farmers do their job even better.

New sprayers help farmers waste fewer chemicals.

# SPRAYER PARTS

chemical tank

cab

nozzle

wheel

boom

NEW HOLLAND

# FUN SPRAYER FACTS

- Small pilotless planes called drones can fly over a field and spot weeds when they are still small. Then farmers can spray just the spots that need herbicide.

- Boom arms on sprayers can be up to 120 feet (37 m) wide! That's as long as a bowling lane.

- Farmers around the world apply about 2 million tons (1.8 million t) of pesticides to their crops every year.

# GLOSSARY

**chemical:** something that is of, relating to, or produced by chemistry

**fertilizer:** a substance or chemical used to help plants grow larger and stronger

**herbicide:** a chemical that kills certain plants

**insecticide:** a chemical that kills certain insects

**mechanical:** having or using machinery

**nozzle:** a spout at the end of a hose or tube

**organic:** raising crops or animals without using human-made chemicals

**self-propelled:** having the ability to move built within the vehicle itself

# FURTHER READING

Dufek, Holly. *A Year on the Farm.* Austin, TX: Octane, 2015.

Maimone, S. M. *Crop Sprayers.* New York: Gareth Stevens, 2017.

Marsico, Katie. *What's It Like to Live Here? Farm.* Ann Arbor, MI: Cherry Lake, 2014.

Mocomi—Organic Farming
http://mocomi.com/organic-farming/

USDA for Kids
https://www.usda.gov/our-agency/initiatives/usda-kids

# EXPLORE MORE

Learn even more about sprayers! Scan the QR code to see photos and videos of sprayers in action.

# INDEX

# PHOTO ACKNOWLEDGMENTS

The images in this book are used with the permission of New Holland except: gorosan/Shutterstock.com, p. 5 (inset); gpointstudio/Shutterstock.com, p. 6; Andres Virviescas/Shutterstock.com, p. 13 (inset); noramin.s/Shutterstock.com, p. 14; Fox Photos/Hulton Archive/Getty Images, p. 16 (inset); Sunny Forest/Shutterstock.com, p. 16 (background); Fox Photos/Hulton Archive/Getty Images, p. 17; Sam Spicer/Shutterstock.com, p. 18; Laura Westlund/Independent Picture Service, p. 23. Design elements: enjoynz/DigitalVision Vectors/Getty Images; CHEMADAN/Shutterstock.com; pingebat/Shutterstock.com; LongQuattro/Shutterstock.com.

Cover: New Holland.